WELCOME TO THE FARM

1

Four-Wheel Drive Utility Tractor

Samantha Bell

Published in the United States of America
by Cherry Lake Publishing
Ann Arbor, Michigan
www.cherrylakepublishing.com

Content Adviser: Gary Powell, Weed Science Research Technician, Michigan State University
Reading Adviser: Marla Conn MS, Ed., Literacy specialist, Read-Ability, Inc.
Photo Credits: © AGCO Corporation, all rights reserved, cover, 1, 2, 8, 12, 16, 20;
© meunierd/Shutterstock, 4; © Karina Gromova/Shutterstock, 6;
© cornfield/Shutterstock, 10; © bogdanhoda/Shutterstock, 14;
© Andy Dean Photography/Shutterstock, 18

Library of Congress Cataloging-in-Publication Data
Names: Bell, Samantha, author. | Bell, Samantha. Welcome to the farm.
Title: Four-wheel drive utility tractor / Samantha Bell.
Description: Ann Arbor : Cherry Lake Publishing, [2016] | Series: Welcome to the farm | Includes bibliographical references and index.
Identifiers: LCCN 2015047230| ISBN 9781634710381 (hardcover) | ISBN 9781634711371 (pdf) | ISBN 9781634712361 (pbk.) | ISBN 9781634713351 (ebook)
Subjects: LCSH: Farm tractors—Juvenile literature. | Four-wheel drive vehicles—Juvenile literature.
Classification: LCC S711 .B418 2016 | DDC 631.3—dc23
LC record available at http://lccn.loc.gov/2015047230

Cherry Lake Publishing would like to acknowledge the work of the Partnership for 21st Century Skills. Please visit www.p21.org for more information.

Printed in the United States of America
Corporate Graphics

Table of Contents

3

Small and Strong

Utility tractors are small and strong. They are used for many things.

They have **four-wheel drive**. They can go up hills. They can go through mud.

What else is in the barn?

They can move in tight spaces. They go in barns. They go under trees.

Grass and Hay

They mow grass and weeds.

Farmers can add tools to the front of the tractor. A shovel scoops soil or hay.

Moving and Pulling

A digger can be attached to the back. It moves dirt and rocks.

Farmers can add many tools to the back. The tractors rake hay and pull **balers**. They pull **plows**.

Backhoes attach to the back of utility tractors. They dig deep holes.

Where does the driver sit?

Big Jobs!

Utility tractors may be small. But they do big jobs!

Find Out More

Dorling Kindersley. *Total Tractor!* New York: DK Publishing, 2015.

John Deere
http://www.deere.com/en_US/media/player/player.html?src=
/ag/58879_01_gep_485abackhoe_hd.mp4&autostart=true
Watch one person add and remove a backhoe to a utility tractor.

Glossary

balers (BAYL-urz) machines that form large bundles of goods
four-wheel drive (FOR-weel DRIVE) a system that applies power
to all four wheels of a vehicle
plows (PLOUZ) machines used to cut and turn over soil
utility (yoo-TIL-i-tee) usefulness

Home and School Connection

Use this list of words from the book to help your child become a better reader. Word games and writing activities can help beginning readers reinforce literacy skills.

a	dig	hay	pallet	things
add	digger	hills	plows	through
and	dirt	holes	pull	tight
are	does	in	pulling	to
attach	drive	is	rake	tools
attached	driver	it	rocks	tractor
back	else	jobs	scoops	tractors
backhoes	farmers	many	shovel	trees
balers	for	may	sit	under
barn	fork	move	small	up
barns	four-wheel	moves	soil	used
big	front	moving	spaces	utility
but	go	mow	strong	weeds
can	grass	mud	the	what
deep	have	of	they	where

Index

About the Author

Samantha Bell is a children's book writer, illustrator, teacher, and mom of four busy kids. Her articles, short stories, and poems have been published online and in print.